# Extreme

# SURFING

### Blaine Wiseman

**Weigl Publishers Inc.**

Published by Weigl Publishers Inc.
350 5th Avenue, Suite 3304, PMB 6G
New York, NY 10118-0069

Website: www.weigl.com
Copyright ©2009 WEIGL PUBLISHERS INC.

All of the Internet URLs given in the book were valid at the time of publication. However, due to the dynamic nature of the Internet, some addresses may have changed, or sites may have ceased to exist since publication. While the author and publisher regret any inconvenience this may cause readers, no responsibility for any such changes can be accepted by either the author or the publisher.

Library of Congress Cataloging-in-Publication Data available upon request.
Fax 1-866-44-WEIGL for the attention of the Publishing Records department.

ISBN 978-1-59036-916-6 (hard cover)
ISBN 978-1-59036-917-3 (soft cover)

Printed in the United States of America
1 2 3 4 5 6 7 8 9 0  12 11 10 09 08

Weigl acknowledges Getty Images as its primary image supplier for this title.
Other credits include Jan Sunn-Carreira: page 29 top right.

Every reasonable effort has been made to trace ownership and to obtain permission to reprint copyright material. The publishers would be pleased to have any errors or omissions brought to their attention so that they may be corrected in subsequent printings.

**EDITOR:** Heather C. Hudak
**DESIGN:** Terry Paulhus
**LAYOUT:** Kathryn Livingstone

# Extreme SURFING

# CONTENTS

# WHAT ARE THE X GAMES?

The X Games are an annual sports tournament that showcases the best athletes in the extreme sports world. Extreme sports are performed at high speeds. Participants must wear special equipment to help protect them from injury. Only athletes who spend years training should take part in these sports. There are many competitions, such as the X Games, that celebrate the skill, dedication, and determination of the athletes, as well as the challenge and difficulty of the sports.

The X Games began as the Extreme Games in 1995. The following year, the name was shortened to X Games. In 1995 and 1996, the games were held in the summer, and they featured a wide variety of sports. These included skateboarding, inline skating, BMX, street luge, sky surfing, and rock climbing.

The popularity of the X Games made it possible for more sports to be showcased. In 1997, the Winter X Games began. The Winter X Games feature sports such as snowboarding, skiing, and snowmobiling. Today, there are Summer and Winter X Games each year.

Some of the best surfers in the world compete in the X Games. These surfers perform extreme moves in front of large crowds on some of the best waves in the world.

## TECHNOLINK

Learn more about the X Games at **expn.go.com**.

# X FEST

The X Games are about more than sports. Each year, musical acts from all over the world perform for fans at the X Games. X Fest is the name for the musical portion of the X Games. It features some of the best-known punk rock, hip hop, and alternative music artists of the time. These artists perform between sporting events and keep the crowds entertained and excited for the competitions.

# WHAT IS SURFING?

**S**urfing is a sport that requires strength, skill, and balance. Surfers stand on a board and ride on top of waves. As the waves push the surfer toward the shore, the surfer rides sideways along them. To get started, surfers swim out into the water, past the **break**. As a wave comes toward the surfers, they lay on their boards and use their arms and feet to paddle toward the shore. When the wave curls over, the surfers stand up on the board.

Surfing is believed to have started in **Polynesia** between 1500 BC and 400 AD. People would surf on top of waves, in canoes, while they were fishing. The Polynesians soon turned this activity into a game. They would lay down on wooden boards and ride the waves. Over time, they learned to stand up on these boards.

## Timeline

**4th Century** AD – People arrive in Hawai'i from Polynesia. They begin surfing sometime during the next 1,000 years.

**1779** – European sailors observe Hawai'ians surfing.

**1901** – The Beach Boys of Waikiki begin giving surf lessons to tourists. This is considered the rebirth of surfing.

**1907** – George Freeth, "The Man Who Can Walk on Water," leaves Hawai'i for California. Freeth becomes the first "California surfer."

**1915** – Duke Paoa Kahanamoku gives a surfing presentation in Sydney, Australia. The sport becomes very popular in that country.

**1928** – The first major surfing contest, the Pacific Coast Surfriding Championships, takes place in Corona del Mar.

Hawai'ians call surfing *he'e nalu*, which means "wave sliding." To early Hawai'ians, he'e nalu was an important part of their culture and religion. It was a training exercise that kept chiefs and royalty in top physical form. Chiefs would display their leadership skills and courage by riding big waves. Hawai'ians also held surfing competitions to settle arguments and conflicts.

**Surfers ride the face, or front part, of a wave.**

As more Europeans arrived in Hawai'i, the local culture changed. Many traditional beliefs and pastimes were replaced by those of Europeans. Surfing declined during this time. However, in the early 1900s, people once again became interested in the sport. A group known as the Beach Boys of Waikiki created a surfing club in the 1970s and reintroduced the sport to locals. After this, surfing spread from Hawai'i to other parts of the world, including California and Australia.

**1950s and 1960s** – New, lighter, less expensive types of surfboards, made of fiberglass and foam, make it easier to ride on waves. Surfing becomes more popular than ever before.

**1969** – Greg Noll surfs a 35-foot (10.7-meter) wave on Hawai'i's North Shore. A new craze, called big wave surfing, begins.

**1998** – Ken Bradshaw surfs a 85-foot (26-m) wave, the biggest wave ever surfed.

**2003** – Surfing becomes part of the X Games in Huntington Beach, California.

# ALL THE RIGHT EQUIPMENT

**E**arly Hawai'ians built surfboards out of native bread-fruit and mahogany trees. As surfing spread around the world at the beginning of the 20th century, surfboard builders continued to use wood native to the area.

These solid-wood boards were as long as 25 feet (7.6 m) and weighed up to 200 pounds (90 kilograms). After World War II, fiberglass and foam were used to make surfboards. These boards were much lighter and could travel faster. Most boards at this time were about 10 feet (3 m) long. In the 1960s, a new board design, called the shortboard, allowed surfers to move faster than ever before and perform new, exciting tricks. These boards were about 6 feet (2 m) long and very lightweight.

Today, longboards and foamboards most often are used by beginner surfers. Longboards are usually about 10 feet (3 m) long and are easier to stand on and ride than shortboards. Foamboards are soft and light. These are the most common type of surfboard.

## ACCESSORIZE IT!

Surf wax is an important accessory for surfers. Rubbing wax into the deck of the board gives it grip. This stops the surfer's feet from slipping while he or she is surfing.

In colder water, a surfer must wear a wetsuit. This is a skin-tight suit that keeps the surfer warm in the water. It is important to choose the right suit for the water conditions.

A leash is connected at one end of the board. The surfer attaches the other end of the leash to his or her ankle. When the surfer falls, the board stays attached to the ankle. This stops the board from being swept away and also helps the surfer stay afloat.

Today, surfboards are made of strong, flexible, lightweight materials, such as polyurethane and epoxy. Most boards have three tail-fins underneath the rear of the board. Fins make the board more stable and easier to control.

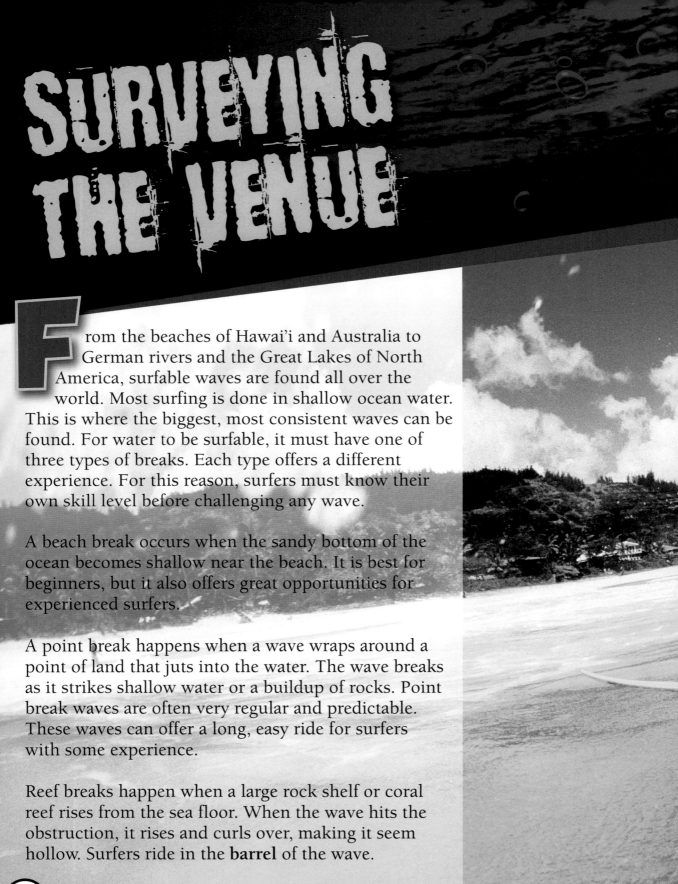

# SURVEYING THE VENUE

From the beaches of Hawai'i and Australia to German rivers and the Great Lakes of North America, surfable waves are found all over the world. Most surfing is done in shallow ocean water. This is where the biggest, most consistent waves can be found. For water to be surfable, it must have one of three types of breaks. Each type offers a different experience. For this reason, surfers must know their own skill level before challenging any wave.

A beach break occurs when the sandy bottom of the ocean becomes shallow near the beach. It is best for beginners, but it also offers great opportunities for experienced surfers.

A point break happens when a wave wraps around a point of land that juts into the water. The wave breaks as it strikes shallow water or a buildup of rocks. Point break waves are often very regular and predictable. These waves can offer a long, easy ride for surfers with some experience.

Reef breaks happen when a large rock shelf or coral reef rises from the sea floor. When the wave hits the obstruction, it rises and curls over, making it seem hollow. Surfers ride in the **barrel** of the wave.

Each wave reacts differently to a break. Knowing how to read the conditions of the water and having the skills to react to changes are important to all surfers.

## TECHNOLINK

To learn more about surfing spots and breaks, visit **www.wannasurf.com**.

# THE GAME—
# MEN'S COMPETITION

Surfing was added to the X Games in 2003. Most surfing competitions take place over many days. However, the X Games are shown on live television, so the organizers needed a surfing event that could be shown in a few hours. They decided to use a competition format called The Game. The Game features two teams of nine surfers competing against each other, and it lasts between two and three hours. Like other televised sports, The Game has coaches, a referee, competing teams, and timeouts.

For the first few years of X Games surfing, teams taking part in The Game came from the east or west coast of the United States. Surfers from the east coast were on the team called East, and west-coast surfers were on the team called West.

Today, The Game includes surfers from all over the world. In this event, American surfers, known as Team USA, compete against surfers from all over the world, called Team World.

During The Game, surfers take three runs, called periods. They are awarded points, out of 10, for each run. At the end of The Game, the scores of all nine surfers are added together. The team that has the most points wins The Game.

Huntington Beach is also known as "Surf City USA®."

## THE GAME—
## MEN'S COMPETITION
## PAST WINNERS

2007
Team USA wins against Team World.

2006
West wins against East.

# THE GAME—
## WOMEN'S COMPETITION

The women's competition was introduced to the X Games in 2007 at Puerto Escondido, Mexico. This competition follows a similar format to The Game that was developed for the men.

This competition features Team USA and Team World battling for the most points. Six women make up each team, with each surfer taking three runs. The event is scored in the same way as the men's competition, with all the scores added together to make up the team's final score. Team USA, coached by Lisa Andersen and led by Melanie Bartels' high score of the day, won the first women's surfing X Games gold medals.

In addition to coaching Team USA at the X Games, Lisa Andersen has taken part in many competitions, including the Roxy Pro at Hossegor, France.

# THE GAME— WOMEN'S COMPETITION PAST WINNERS

2007
Team USA wins against
Team World.

# THE GAME—
## LOCAL'S COMPETITION

**E**ach year, the X Games allows local athletes to become a part of the X Games experience. Local surfers are given a chance to show off their skills in front of the best surfers in the world.

The Local's event features two teams of surfers from the host area competing against each other in The Game. Six surfers make up each team. Two team captains are chosen, and all other competitor's names are drawn from a hat. The coaches from the men's competition help coach the locals. In 2007, Los Tiburones, or The Sharks, faced off against Las Malaguas, The Jellyfish, in Puerto Escondido, Mexico. Los Tiburones team captain David Rutherford impressed the professionals with his sportsmanship and skills. Team World coach Martin Potter invited Rutherford to play in their match against Team USA.

Prior to coaching Team World, Martin Potter was a world-class surfer.

Puerto Escondido is also known as "the Mexican Pipeline."

# THE GAME— LOCAL'S COMPETITION PAST WINNERS

2007
Los Tiburones win against Las Malaguas.

2006
The Aztecas win against the Mayas.

# QUALIFYING TO COMPETE

**A**ll professional surfers have one thing in common—they are sponsored. Being sponsored means that surfboard manufacturers, clothing companies, magazines, surf shops, and other surfing companies give a surfer free clothes, equipment, and money. In return, the sponsored surfer must wear that company's clothes, ride its board, and endorse its products. Getting sponsored is the best way to become a professional surfer.

## TECHNOLINK

To learn more about getting sponsored, visit **www.surfspono.com**.

The first step to finding a sponsor is getting noticed for your surfing skills. Sponsors or team leaders are often looking for up-and-coming surfers at the beach. Surfing as much as possible, having fun, and improving one's skills are the best ways to get noticed.

Another great way to showcase a person's skills is through a **portfolio**. A portfolio is a collection of facts, pictures, and video footage of surfing moves. This is proof of a surfer's skills. A **resume** can be included in a portfolio.

Then, make contact with surfing companies. Look on company websites, talk to local professionals, and ask at local surf shops about getting sponsored. Send the portfolio to these companies, or bring it to a local shop. This is all a part of getting noticed.

Making it to the X Games as a surfer is different than all other sports. In other X Games sports, athletes must perform well in competitions throughout the year in order to qualify. Surfing is the only X Games sport that is played in a team format, so the coaches of each team choose the surfers that will compete. Surfers must surf well enough throughout the year to impress the coaches. Coaches do not focus on a surfer's overall points at competitions. X Games surfers are chosen for the quality of their surfing, skills, sportsmanship, and ability to work in a team environment.

While surfing is a unique sport that is popular around the world, it is not the only sport where the athlete rides a board. These sports are similar to surfing.

## Skateboarding

Skateboarding is a sport that was invented by surfers. Wheels attached to the bottom of a wooden board allowed surfers to surf on land. The sport became popular in the 1970s, and it is now one of the fastest growing sports in the world.

Skateboarding is most popular in cities and towns where there is a large amount of concrete and pavement. City streets offer a wide variety of obstacles where stunts and tricks can be performed. Skateparks have become common in cities. They offer a place for skaters to have fun in their own environment. Great skateboarding cities include Barcelona, San Francisco, Vancouver, and Sao Paulo.

## Snowboarding

Snowboarding is a combination of surfing and skiing. Snowboarders ride a board down a snow-covered hill at very high speeds. Since the mid-1990s, snowboarding has become a well-known sport around the world. World-class snowboarding hills can be found in Utah, the Canadian Rockies, the Swiss Alps, and the mountains of New Zealand.

## Kiteboarding

In kiteboarding, the athlete is tied to a specially designed kite, while his or her feet are strapped to a board. The kites catch much more wind than regular kites, pulling the rider along at speeds of 48 **knots** per hour. Kiteboarding is most commonly done on water. However, it can also be done on snow, dirt, and pavement. Top kiteboarding spots include California, Mexico, The Bahamas, and Vietnam.

## Wakeboarding

Wakeboarding is a mix of both surfing and water skiing. Like surfing, the athlete rides a board in the water. He or she holds onto a rope that is attached to a motorboat. The boat tows the wakeboarder through the water at high speeds. The rider uses the **wake** as a jump and performs **aerial** stunts behind the boat. Wakeboarding can be done on almost any smooth body of water where motorboats are allowed. Some of the best places for wakeboarding are California, Costa Rica, Australia, and Greece.

# UNFORGETTABLE MOMENTS

Throughout the history of the X Games, there have been many unforgettable moments. Some of the most memorable times focus on close competitions where no one could foresee which team would win until the very end.

The 2003 and 2004 X Games surfing competitions were held at Huntington Beach, California. While Huntington Beach, also known as "Surf City," is a very popular place to surf, it did not offer the world-class waves that X Games surfers and organizers hoped for. During the first X Games surf contest, 25,000 fans watched as Team East and Team West battled for top spot. Small but powerful waves ripped through the water. The crowd went crazy as the surfers practiced their best moves while preparing for the event.

To begin, Team East pulled out high scores. Team West tried to compete, but they could not catch a good wave. In round two, the points separating the two teams narrowed, as the waves started rolling in for the West. The East secured a big lead with great rides in the third quarter, and the waves once again stopped rolling for the West. Just as the East thought they had gripped the win, the West started scoring big. Dane Reynolds, the youngest surfer, scored top points of the day. Luck stayed on the side of Team East. Despite their best efforts, the lack

of solid waves kept the West from making any more big moves, and Team East won the gold.

Women's surfing joined the X Games in 2007. The man who invented The Game, Brad Gerlach, said the first women's competition was the most exciting game he had seen. Team USA won the gold medal by beating Team World with the smallest spread of points—three—in X Games surfing history. Melanie Bartels of Team USA had the wave of the day, scoring 8.5 out of 10.

# AROUND THE WORLD

## Oahu, United States

Hawai'i is the home of surfing, and the island of Oahu offers some of the best surf spots in the world. Pipeline, Waimea Bay, or Outer Log Cabins are legendary for their extreme conditions. The waves at these places are a challenge for the best surfers in the world. Oahu also offers many other spots that are great for learning or gaining experience.

*ATLANTIC OCEAN*

## Santa Catarina Island, Brazil

Santa Catarina Island in southern Brazil is well known for its surf. Surf spots such as Barra da Lagoa offer great small waves for beginners and experienced surfers. World-class spots such as Praia Joaquina, which has stadium lights for night surfing, are used by more experienced surfers.

**1**

**2**

*PACIFIC OCEAN*

## Tahiti, French Polynesia

Tahiti is the perfect place for surfers. Crystal clear water, excellent beaches, and some of the best waves in the world attract surfers to this small island. Teahupoo is known for having some of the most dangerous waves in the world, but Tahiti has many other spots with barreling waves that guarantee the surfing experience of a lifetime.

# Games Venues

ARCTIC
OCEAN

ARCTIC
OCEAN

## Donegal Bay, Ireland

Ireland is well known for its green hills, music, and friendly people. In recent years, it has become popular with surfers. Donegal Bay, on the west coast of the island, attracts surfers who do not mind surfing in cold water. Mullaghmore and Bundoran get very large waves, for experienced surfers only, while Easkey is a great place for surfers of all skill levels.

## Jeffrey's Bay, South Africa

Jeffrey's Bay is the best known surfing area in all of Africa. All levels of surfer can surf at Jeffrey's Bay. Seal Point and Supertubes are two spots for experienced surfers only, while all levels can surf at Cape Saint Francis and The Point.

PACIFIC
OCEAN

INDIAN
OCEAN

## Gold Coast, Australia

Australia's Gold Coast is so well known for its surf that one of its beaches is named Surfer's Paradise. This beach is the perfect spot for beginners, offering small waves and a surfing school. More experienced surfers can try their moves at other breaks, including Burleigh Heads, Kirra, or Nobby's Beach.

25

# CURRENT STARS

## KELLY SLATER

**HOMETOWN**
Cocoa Beach, Florida,
United States

**BORN**
February 11, 1972

**NOTES**
Has won eight World
Championships—the most
in history

Was the youngest World Champion,
at 20 years old, in 1992, and the
oldest, at 34, in 2006

Scored a world-record two perfect
runs for a score of 20 out of 20 at
Teahupoo in 2006

## LAYNE BEACHLEY

**HOMETOWN**
Sydney, New South
Wales, Australia

**BORN**
May 24, 1972

**NOTES**
Has won seven
World Championships

In 2003, won Female Athlete
of the Year in Australia

Became a professional surfer
without ever competing in an
**amateur** competition

# LAIRD HAMILTON

**HOMETOWN**
North Shore Oahu,
Hawai'i, United States

**BORN**
March 2, 1964

**NOTES**
Adopted by legendary surfer Billy Hamilton in 1966

Developed **tow-in surfing** in 1992 and is the best-known big wave surfer

Produces his own surfing videos and has appeared in Hollywood movies, such as *Die Another Day*

# ROCHELLE BALLARD

**HOMETOWN**
Kauai, Hawai'i,
United States

**BORN**
February 13, 1971

**NOTES**
Was part of the first-ever women's X Games gold medal surfing team in 2007

Was the first president of International Women's Surfing, an organization promoting women's surfing around the world

Appeared in the Hollywood movie *Blue Crush* and surf videos *Step Into Liquid* and *The Modus Mix*

# LEGENDS

## DUKE PAOA KAHANAMOKU

**HOMETOWN**
Waikiki, Hawai'i,
United States

**BORN**
August 24, 1890

**NOTES**
Introduced surfing
to Australia

Won three Olympic gold medals
and one silver medal for swimming

Known as "The Father
of Modern Surfing"

## TOM BLAKE

**HOMETOWN**
Milwaukee, Wisconsin,
United States

**BORN**
March 8, 1902

**NOTES**
Was inspired to surf in
1920, after seeing an
exhibition by Duke
Kahanamoku in
Detroit, Michigan

Invented the hollow
surfboard, surfboard fins,
and surf photography

Is only the second
person honored in both
the swimming and
surfing halls of fame,
along with Duke
Kahanamoku

# LINDA BENSON

**HOMETOWN**
Encinitas, California, United States

**BORN**
Unknown

**NOTES**
U.S. surf champion in 1959, 1960, 1961, 1964, and 1968

Surfed as a Hollywood stunt person

Was the youngest International Women's Champion, at 15 years old

# RELL SUNN

**HOMETOWN**
Makaha, Hawai'i, United States

**BORN**
July 31, 1950

**NOTES**
Middle name, *Kapolioka'ehukai*, means "Heart of the Sea" in Hawai'ian

Hawai'i's first full-time female lifeguard

Helped start the Women's Professional Surfing Association

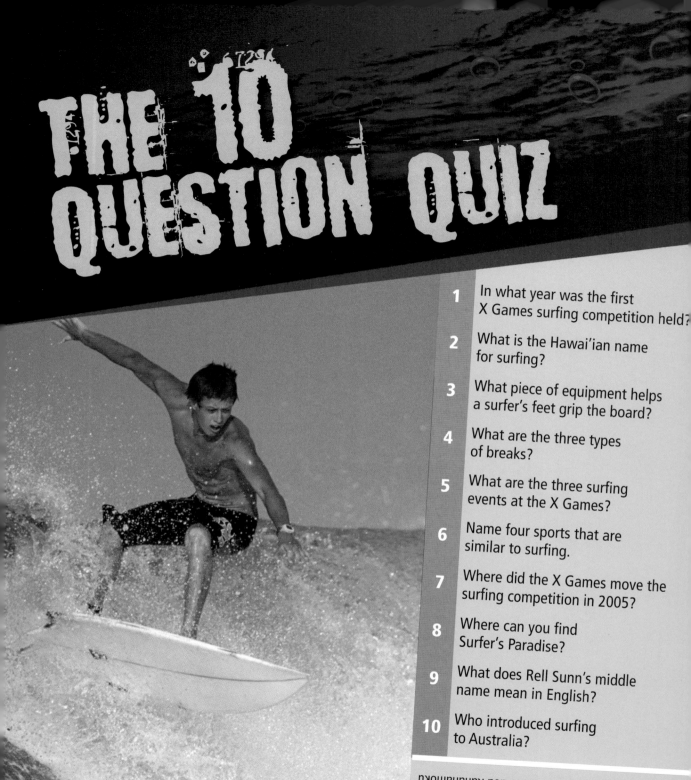

# THE 10 QUESTION QUIZ

1. In what year was the first X Games surfing competition held?

2. What is the Hawai'ian name for surfing?

3. What piece of equipment helps a surfer's feet grip the board?

4. What are the three types of breaks?

5. What are the three surfing events at the X Games?

6. Name four sports that are similar to surfing.

7. Where did the X Games move the surfing competition in 2005?

8. Where can you find Surfer's Paradise?

9. What does Rell Sunn's middle name mean in English?

10. Who introduced surfing to Australia?

**Answers:** 1. 2003 2. He'e nalu 3. surf wax 4. Beach, Point, and Reef 5. Men's, Women's, and Local's 6. Skateboarding, Snowboarding, Kiteboarding, and Wakeboarding 7. Puerto Escondido, Mexico 8. Gold Coast, Australia 9. "Heart of the Sea " 10. Duke Paoa Kahanamoku

# RESEARCH

www.expn.go.com/srf

www.surfline.com

www.surfing-waves.com

http://dsc.discovery.com/games/
surfing/surfing.html

Many books and websites provide information on surfing. To learn more, borrow books from the library, or surf the Internet.

Most libraries have computers that connect to a database for researching information. If you input a keyword, you will be provided with a list of books in the library that contain information on that topic. Nonfiction books are arranged numerically, using their call number. Fiction books are organized alphabetically by the author's last name.

# GLOSSARY INDEX

**aerial:** taking place in the air

**amateur:** a person who is not paid to do a sport

**barrel:** the hollow inside a breaking wave; sometimes called a tube

**break:** to curl over or fall apart in the foam of waves

**knots:** measurements of speed for travel on a body of water

**Polynesia:** one of three main groups of islands in the Pacific

**portfolio:** a collection or sampling of one's work

**resume:** a document that has an overview of one's training, skills, and experience in a certain area

**tow-in surfing:** when a surfer is pulled by a boat or helicopter into a wave

**wake:** a wave made by a boat moving through the water